WHAT RESPECTED LEADERS
ARE SAYING ABOUT THIS BOOK

"Dr. Audi's good examples and practical tips help me enjoy my work. Here's your own opportunity to learn how to enjoy your work as well."

—BARBARA WILLIS
Chief Operating Officer, Detroit Rescue Mission

"I love the clarity, consistency and conviviality of this book by Dr. Chad Audi, and I hope target readers will find it resourceful and rejuvenating."

—DR. PAUL EDISON
CEO, Apollos University
Great Falls, Montana

"With the helpful tips in this book, you can regain your enthusiasm and dedication to the work you do. So, why wait? Start reading."

—RANDALL A. PENTIUK, ESQ
Managing Partner
Pentiuk, Couvreur & Kobiljak, P.C.
Board Chair, Detroit Rescue Mission Ministries

"This book is as straight to the point as Dr. Chad Audi himself, whose wisdom will enrich the lives of his readers, both professionally and personally."

—ERIC SCHEIBLE, ESQ.
Partner
Frasco Caponigro Wineman & Scheible, PLLC

"When I read Dr. Audi's manuscript, it was clear to me that he is a purposeful, accessible and considerate leader who carries his team along. That's not common these days. I hope all my students and partners in human capacity development would enjoy reading this motivational book."

—WILLIAMS EMEKA OBIOZOR, ED.D.
Professor, Nnamdi Azikiwe University
Awka, Nigeria
Rector, Nation Builders College
of Technology, Asaba, Nigeria

"A great roadmap for all of us who have had, or are having, or will have 'bad days.' "

—MIKE SMITH
Johanna Meijer Magoon Principal Archivist (Retd.)
Bentley Historical Library
The University of Michigan

"As a registered nurse and serial entrepreneur, I appreciate and commend this book's mission of helping me with practical tips to keep my morale high at all times. I think other readers will find it helpful too."

—CHARMAINE BOND
CEO, Pure Apparel &
Gold Standard Massage Clinic

"Dr. Audi has done a wonderful job putting together these experience-based and heartfelt recommendations for enjoying your work again. So, no more excuses."

—HONORABLE RAED CHARAFEDDINE
First Vice-Governor, Lebanon's Central Bank
Alternate Governor for Lebanon
at the International Monetary Fund

"This commendable work empowers workers to prioritize and pursue their own motivation."

—ANTHONY HOLT
Associate Vice President & Chief of Police
Wayne State University, Detroit

7 KEYS
TO ENJOYING
YOUR WORK
AGAIN

CHAD AUDI, PH.D.

Art by
LUBA LUKOVA

clay & gold

ISBN-13: 978-0-9788372-6-6
ISBN-10: 0-9788372-6-6

Art © Luba Lukova, www.lukova.net
Photographs courtesy of DRMM

First published 2019
by Clay & Gold
3105 Crescent Street, Long Island City, New York 11106, USA
www.clayandgold.com

Typeset in Sibon and Interstate
Printed and bound in the United States of America

Dedicated to the men and women who put in their best efforts at work and get the best results.

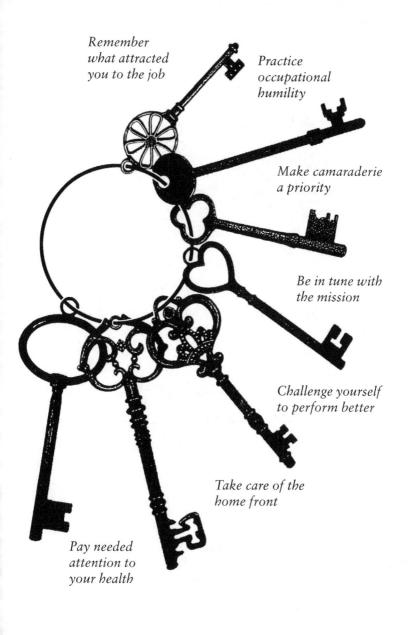

Remember what attracted you to the job

Practice occupational humility

Make camaraderie a priority

Be in tune with the mission

Challenge yourself to perform better

Take care of the home front

Pay needed attention to your health

CONTENTS

FOREWORD

I'm going to follow Dr. Chad Audi's advice and be transparent with you. The first question you should ask yourself is: why should I read another book that portends to tell me how to cope with a life situation?

Well, there is a simple answer: read it because Dr. Audi has written a fine book that will indeed help you with a common life situation, enjoying your work again. There are legions of people that face workplace problems every day, and in this respect, not one of us can say that we have never had a "bad" day, a day when we take no joy in our work. This is one of the most common issues facing any working person.

So, what do we do about this, and why is Dr. Audi the person to give us ideas that we can embrace? Does this book matter?

First, I can tell you that, in my professional career, I have met thousands of people from all walks of life. Although I have held a number of blue-collar jobs and spent time in the United States Marine Corps, after earning several college degrees, the bulk of my career has been spent working for a university.

Of all the people I have met, none has impressed me more than Dr. Audi, President and CEO of the Detroit Rescue Mission. In this capacity, he works in a very tough professional field, managing a large non-profit organization that, every single day of the year, engages with and directly assists thousands of the most disadvantaged citizens in one of the most impoverished large cities in America.

In short, every day, Dr. Audi, with his own eyes, sees people with troubles. Yet, he is always upbeat and affable. And, every day, Dr. Audi has to manage his organization, which faces the same internal issues in terms of administrative and human resource problems that a company like General Motors or Amazon has to deal with, but since he manages a non-profit that depends on sometimes-undependable support from state and local governments, grants and donations, it is a tougher slough. Yet, he always seems to enjoy his work, is open-minded, and eager for progress.

How does he do it?

I remember seeing a billboard on Seven Mile Road in Detroit that had a caricature of famous, long-serving mayor of the city, Coleman Young, along with one of his favorite sayings: "You can't look backward and forward at the same time." While this is a common sense approach to the world, it is an approach based on undeniable logic. Dr. Audi embodies this philosophy and always looks forward. Which brings us to the *7 Keys to Enjoying Your Work Again*, a brief but succinct piece of prose that is forward thinking from start to finish.

In the *7 Keys*, Dr. Audi tackles a common problem for just about every working person in America. No matter what work one does for a living, there are moments, or days, or weeks or longer, where we lose our enthusiasm for our work. While this is a common issue, it is not a common theme for the plethora of self-help or motivational or similar works currently on the book market.

Dr. Audi tackles the issue, demonstrating that he is the type of person and chief administrator who spends some serious time and effort thinking about such singular human issues. He does so in order to move himself and his organization forward.

This is also a book that is written from Dr. Audi's vast personal and highly successful experience in humanistic affairs. It is also a book written from his kind heart.

When, for example, he urges the reader in Chapter Five to "Challenge Yourself to Perform Better", it is because he challenges himself and his colleagues every day. Or, in Chapter Two, when Dr. Audi believes we should "Make Camaraderie A Priority," it is because he cares about his own comrades at the Detroit Rescue Mission and does his best to see to their well-being. Indeed, as you will see, this is certainly his motivation for Chapter Six "Take Care of the Home Front," and Chapter Seven, "Pay Needed Attention to Your Health."

But, make no mistake about it – the 7 *Keys* is not a work of "pie-in-the-sky," wishful idealism that provides solutions for a world that we wish existed but does not. It is a book grounded in reality. Dr. Audi recognizes that, in any given occupation, there are forces that are beyond any employee's control: uncaring bosses or disenchanted colleagues, or just plain tough duties and responsibilities. To say nothing of forces outside of the workplace that affect an organization's culture and atmosphere, or personal issues on the home front that are carried into the office.

Not every job has the same joy years after the first day. Practical advice on how to cope with circumstances, and even excel, is the essence of the 7 *Keys*. Dr. Audi provides some solid, practical suggestions for enjoying work, as well as success and satisfaction in one's professional endeavors.

Finally, when thinking about the 7 *Keys,* I can safely say, yes, Dr. Audi's work matters, and it can help us in our daily lives. Simply put, the 7 *Keys* is a great roadmap for all of us who have had, or are having, or will have "bad days."

Whenever you are having one – Dr. Audi does state that we all have them (although it is hard to believe that he has ever had a bad day!) – you'll be happy you have the *7 Keys* on your bookshelf and can read it again. And that is the mark of great books with great ideas from someone who has devoted himself to the study of the human spirit. This is one of those books.

MIKE SMITH
Johanna Meijer Magoon
Principal Archivist (Retd.)
Bentley Historical Library
The University of Michigan

"Change does not roll in on the wheels of inevitability, but comes through continuous struggle.

—Dr. Martin Luther King, Jr.
Civil rights icon and Nobel Peace laureate

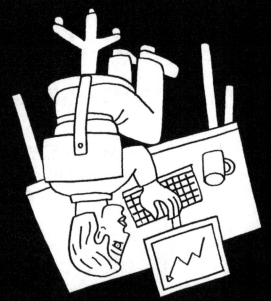

The old expression goes "a journey of a thousand miles begins with one step." That is true. You have to start somewhere. But consider how impracticable it is to complete such a long journey without taking time to refuel, stretch the legs, and refresh the body before continuing on. It could prove dangerous, even debilitating.

When looked at closely, remunerated work, be it in public service, business or nonprofit, is not that different. It, too, is a long journey of creating, innovating and maintaining value. Yet, at one point or another, for varying reasons, people tend to lose interest. Their commitment wanes. Even when they depend on the job to pay bills and support their family.

This doesn't only happen to low wage earners at menial jobs. Long-serving managers, even top executives, can at times, lose interest and commitment.

I have been at the helm of a large nonprofit organization since the late '90s, and I would be lying if I told you I've never been demoralized, disappointed or doubtful. There are times I wonder if I should continue doing all in my power to provide hope and help to the homeless, hungry and hurting of metro Detroit. There are times I ask myself if my sacrifices would have made a greater difference in another sector. There are times I feel like considering the compelling job offers that occasionally come in from other organizations.

I am only human. I get demotivated at times–just like my employees do. But then I quickly remember that my work is not yet done. I embrace routines that refresh my vision, and rekindle my passion and commitment.

Wouldn't it be nice if all employees could maintain the enthusiasm they had on their first day of work? Wouldn't it be awesome if demotivation were only a matter of imagination?

But it is real. In fact, a 2006 Harvard Management Update study goes as far as saying "The fault lies squarely at the feet of management – both the policies and procedures companies employ in managing their workforces and in the relationships that individual managers establish with their direct reports."[1] Thus, the

1.   David Sirota, Louis A. Mischkind, and Michael Irwin Meltzer, "Why Your Employees Are Losing Motivation", Authorized reprint from "Stop Demotivating Your Employees!" *Harvard Management Update*, Vol. 11, No. 1, January, 2006. https://hbswk.hbs.edu/archive/why-your-employees-are-losing-motivation, accessed November, 2018.

writers argue, the task of employers is not to motivate employees but to stop demotivating them.

What if, instead of pointing the finger, we explored ways of helping the employees enjoy their work again?

In a nutshell, that's what this quick-read is about.

If you've ever wondered how I get myself going after the difficult challenges of working with the underprivileged, this book is for you. And if you've ever thought I–or any other well-known top executive–effortlessly bounce back and achieve more because we are somehow superhuman, this book says it's none of that; it's about knowing and applying the right keys.

There are no magic wands in this book. But I do carefully dust off what has worked for me and what has gotten me here so far. Dr. Martin Luther King, Jr. put it best thus: "If we are to go forward, we must go back and rediscover these precious values–that all reality hinges on moral foundations and that all reality has spiritual control."

It's easy to say you are going to start over. It's harder to do. Too often, we fall into bad habits, and eventually become bad workers. We start coming to work late, leaving work too early, being present but less productive, and distracting and discouraging others from doing what they are supposed to do and do well – while continuing to receive their fortnightly or monthly pay. How good is that?

This book is here to help them to start enjoying their work again.

Having served in the for-profit and nonprofit sectors for over two decades, I know that disinterested and dysfunctional employees can be toxic. They underperform and encourage others to underperform with them. They easily find fault, even with things they had previously praised. And they are quick to blame others.

To them, the problem is always with their superiors, subordinates or coordinates. They are never at fault. And the longer they stay in that frame of mind, the more damage they cause themselves, colleagues and the organization at large.

You might think this makes them bad people. Not at all. It makes them people who need refreshing. Who need to start enjoying their work again. Who need to feel they are making an impact.

Is your work fun? Is it a source of pride and joy to you? Do you get the feeling that you are there for such a time as this? Do you look forward to arriving at work early?

If not, the journey of making your work fun again starts now. But mind you, fun doesn't mean easy, and enjoying something doesn't necessarily mean it is effortless or non-demanding. Ultimately, we enjoy what we value, and we value what we invest in.

I will talk about all of this – and more – in the ensuing chapters.

So, please, turn the page...

CHAPTER 1

REMEMBER WHAT ATTRACTED YOU TO THE JOB

"We all want progress, but if you're on the wrong road, progress means doing an about-turn and walking back to the right road...

—C. S. Lewis
British theologian, academic and writer

I am blessed to have a number of highly skilled people who have worked with me for over a decade. I see them as family.

When they inform me each year of their work anniversary, I often flash back to the day they were hired. I remember their infectious enthusiasm and try to figure if it has increased or decreased, and why.

Let's face it. People work for different reasons. In the best cases, there is a personal motivation. A child who lost his parents to cancer may choose to study oncology, just as a child who grew up in a foster home may go into the field of social work. Both are likely to feel a sense of purpose, even destiny, in their chosen career.

However, the common refrain in our society is "Go to school so you can go to college, so you can get a diploma and earn a good-paying job to pay your bills and take care of your family."

I heard this many times. Likely you did as well. So, despite your personal interests, you may find yourself applying for a job mostly for financial reasons. This is why interviewers ask questions like, "Why do you want this job?" and "Why should we hire you?" If all you say in response is "I want to pay my bills," chances are that you won't be hired.

And if, by a stroke of luck, you are hired, you might still feel demotivated once inflation or a change in your consumption patterns finds your salary below your bills.

Thankfully, although I needed money like everyone else, something different brought me to my nonprofit life back in 1997.

I had actually secured a dream job with a major corporation. It was not to start for a few months. In the interim, someone suggested I volunteer my finance and management skills at a nonprofit that was in financial distress. I hadn't heard the name Detroit Rescue Mission before. Curious, and with time to spare, I knocked on its door, offering to volunteer.

Within a few weeks, the long-serving president and CEO, Don DeVos, noticed I was a good asset, and he offered me full-time employment. It was awkward. I wasn't as interested in the nonprofit world as I was in the for-profit world. And besides, the pay was far less than what I would get at the big corporation.

In the end, two things convinced me to let the big job go and sign on with the Rescue Mission, which had been founded back in 1909:

1. My dad, an international corporate executive, had a lengthy phone conversation with Mr. DeVos, and advised me to accept the job offer; he said working with the organization would provide a priceless experience, and the chance to touch lives in a meaningful way; and

2. Mr. DeVos invited me to attend an event in which a teacher with master's degree explained how DRMM helped save her from the dungeons of drug addiction and its attendant financial ruin, job loss and homelessness.

I needed no further convincing. I accepted the job with the lower pay. The rest is history.

That was over 20 years ago. I am still working for that same difference-making organization. And we serve and positively transform more needy people today than we did when I joined.

Why is this personal story important?

Here's why: Whenever I get discouraged, frustrated,

whenever I get the slightest urge to leave this organization for a more lucrative financial position, I remember the very important considerations that made me join it in the first place.

I remember my dad's precious words of advice. And the words of that former school teacher whose life was saved. And I bounce back. I become energized and enthusiastic to work even harder and smarter with my team, to take our organization to the next level.

So now I ask you: what attracted you to your current employer? What made you decide to work for that organization?

Was it community impact?

Name recognition?

The remuneration package?

The team spirit?

The staff development?

The fact that your best friend works there?

Proximity to your home?

The friendly disposition of a supervisor?

The list goes on. Everyone has something special that got them to sign on. You must remember yours and appreciate it once again, even if things are not exactly as they used to be. Change happens – and should happen – in all organizations.

In many ways, enjoying your work again is akin to falling in love with your spouse again. You start from the beginning, by mentally recreating those resplendent ab initio moments when it seemed as if the whole world stood still for both of you.

And before you know it, your marital relationship feels fresh. You rediscover the spark. And you will appreciate what drew you together in the first place.

Now, don't get me wrong. Satisfaction may start there but it doesn't end there. Other things may be needed to return to the path of enjoying your work again.

Such as?

Let's go to the next chapter.

CHAPTER 2

*PRACTICE
OCCUPATIONAL
HUMILITY*

"Humility is the mother of all virtues. If you are humble, nothing will touch you, neither praise nor disgrace, because you know what you are. If you are blamed, you will not be discouraged. If they call you a saint, you will not put yourself on a pedestal.

—MOTHER TERESA
*Nobel Peace laureate and
founder Missionaries of Charity*

The Good Book tells the story of two brothers, James and John, who asked to have the choicest positions in heaven. Their colleagues were indignant but their wise Boss defused the tension, and took the opportunity to teach all of them to be humble, servant leaders.

I think of that compelling story whenever I am faced with a situation that is contrary to occupational humility.

When you have many people working in an organization, it is likely that few of them will see themselves as better than others. They may treat others with disrespect, as if they are undeserving of dignity or reward. This happens in families, communities, even places of worship. It is part of human folly.

And ego.

Now, it is a good and commendable thing if you are among the best and brightest. There is nothing condemnable about being at the top. I am yet to come across anybody who likes to celebrate mediocrity. We should all aspire to be the best that we can be in whatever we do. For the most part, excellence attracts and mediocrity repels.

However, some so-called top players can be very prideful at work. This may be a result of the praise they received for their well-dressed efforts. Instead of focusing on improving their work, they tend to dwell in their self-importance and indispensability. And this can make them complacent. Their performance stagnates or declines. Frustration sets in. Those who used to hold them in high regard begin to see them as unworthy of their position and pay.

In the last 20 years, I have hired some of the most qualified and experienced men and women in their field, with CVs as long as the Mississippi River. But I can tell you that some of them did not acquit themselves well. I expected so much from them. Instead, I got fanciful excuses, pie in the sky answers, and perennial suggestions to hire more people to assist them.

Is that not occupational pride hiding in plain sight? Though they think and act as if they are the best, their outputs suggest the contrary. They may start off by creating the perception that they are untouchable. But before long, their non-performance exposes them as vulnerable, insecure and unhappy.

Note of caution: It is not that they are bad people. They are often people of good intentions and aspirations. They, too, desire the best for the organization, but their outputs are far less than the image they parade.

For me, the best testament to one's knowledge, experience and potentials is a good outcome. That's it. When people boast about big CVs, I expect big and difference-making results from them. If they don't produce such, they need to rethink, rejuvenate and refocus. They need to invite into their lives a good old friend named humility.

More often than not, humility sets in through bare-knuckle, rigorous and dispassionate self-evaluation. It begins to form when we tell ourselves the difficult truth. When we admit our limitations.

When we realize that despite our top knowledge and experience, there are many vital things we do not yet know.

I am sure you've heard the buzzwords "unlearn" and "relearn". They are important in practicing occupational humility. Some fancy knowledge can act like plaque, clogging the inner walls of performance.

Therefore, we need to "unlearn" that kind of knowledge and go for the kind that will not only clear the plaque, but ensure our work heart beats well.

Are colleagues resisting and frustrating you? It might be that they see you as proud and/or dismissive of their contributions. Be intentionally humble and you will reap its fruits. This does not mean working in isolation, threading timidly or allowing people to walk all over you.

No. Being intentionally humble means accepting the fact that your knowledge and experience are not absolute. It means acknowledging mistakes when you make them and making appropriate efforts to correct them. It means seeking and learning new ways to do better and achieve better. It means being open and receptive to better ideas. It means recognizing and appreciating the knowledge and experience of others. It means being self-confident without treating others condescendingly.

You can start here and now, and keep at it daily. There is so much to gain by working humbly—better relationships with colleagues, better application of one's strength, improved performance, and so on.

An old king was asked to disclose the secret of peace and progress in his mid-sized kingdom, and he said "cultivation of mutual respect and consideration." That is instructive, particularly the word "cultivation," which connotes a process, a journey, a continuous effort – just like the word practice.

Occupational humility is something to cultivate. It's like that beautiful flower you have to water daily. Of course, akin to occupational humility is camaraderie, which is next on the list.

CHAPTER **3** *MAKE
CAMARADERIE
A PRIORITY*

"A tree only makes a forest in the mind of a smug.

—C. PASCHAL EZE
*American writer and
board chair The PuLSE Institute*

Like Bob or Betty who works hard and smart to earn a living, I invest the better part of my day in my charity work that spans five Michigan counties.

Forget the 9 am – 5 pm orthodoxy. I work an average of 14 hours a day. Think weekends are off-limits? Wrong. I work weekends and public holidays too. Even while on vacation overseas, I carry the strategic and tactical weight of the organization on my shoulders, remaining in touch with my senior staff members.

Many presidents and CEOs around the world will tell you their work never ends at a set time. They don't clock in and out. They can't.

You can imagine how stressful this is. Perhaps your work is the same. I usually advise job seekers to run from any recruiter that promises a job without stress. They can't be telling the truth.

The real challenge, however, is handling the stress well enough that it does not hinder one's productivity. This is where camaraderie comes in.

We all need to create, sustain and enjoy "mutual trust and friendship" with the people we spend many hours with each day. If we don't, our work will be boring, frustrating, and certainly more stressful.

Those who work directly with me will tell you I am open and transparent to them, and I expect nothing less from them. We freely discuss issues of mutual concern to us as part of the priceless human assets of the organization. They know my vision and plans. They have no doubt where I am taking the organization. They also know what I expect of them in that journey.

But our conversations are not confined to issues relating to the organization. I have outside challenges that I share with them, and I encourage them to freely discuss theirs with me. Together, we explore and find solutions. That's what those in "mutual trust and friendship" do.

As I often say, despite our differing designations and responsibilities, we are all family, and family members help each other.

That aside, the nature of today's work environment is such that nobody can be an island. Even home-based business owners cannot run their businesses alone. They need helpful and trusted coaches and mentors, web designers, bookkeepers, courier service providers, printers, auto mechanics, and so on.

These service providers may not be on the monthly or biweekly payroll, but a trust and friendly relationship with them is needed to keep the business going and the business owner "sane." In other words, nobody succeeds alone. We all need good and healthy relationships for our purposes and projects to succeed.

One of my senior staff members often marvels at how accessible I am as president and CEO, and I readily explain to him that being accessible makes me human. Being accessible enhances my situational awareness and analysis, objectivity, empathy and decision making.

I also humbly add that even the Lord God Almighty is easily accessible to us through prayer and study of his "ancient words." We don't have to do a special ritual or religious gymnastics to approach him. He loves us and wants us to trust him and have the best from him.

We won't have that by keeping our distance, right?

So, if the all-powerful God is that accessible, why shouldn't humans follow suit? Reaching out to others can help us identify with their needs.

Perhaps, you can now see why I noted in the previous

chapter that professional humility and camaraderie are closely related. To borrow the words of late United States senator and vice president, Hubert H. Humphrey, "This, then, is the test we must set for ourselves; not to march alone but to march in such a way that others will wish to join us."

Yes, our routine and spontaneous actions either define and draw others to us as partners and friends working together to achieve a common objective, which is lovely, or pull them away from us as rejects and roadblocks, which is terrible.

It may seem trivial that I remember and celebrate the birthdays of staff members who work directly with me at our head offices in Detroit but I have found it very rewarding. Besides, they remember and celebrate mine as well.

As the saying goes, "It is not about the size or value of the gifts, it is the thought that counts." The thought that your co-worker deserves to be appreciated and celebrated on their special day is certainly invaluable. People of all backgrounds and circumstances place high premium on kind words and gestures, which tend to draw them closer to us both in semblance and in substance.

That brings me to this simple question: how do you treat those who work with you? As co-assets or as dispensable liabilities? The way you treat them plays a huge role in how you feel about your work. In other words, you are more likely to enjoy your work if you treat your co-workers with respect and dignity – which they are likely to reciprocate. Good begets good and evil begets evil.

If you desire to enjoy your work, you should not only seek what's best for you but also seek what's best for those you work with. When you do, and they reciprocate, the workplace becomes a lot of fun, despite the unavoidable challenges and stress.

I enjoy sharing jokes at times with my staff. I enjoy laughing aloud at work even when things are tough. I enjoy the opportunity to break bread with them. I enjoy pulling dark or milk chocolate from my drawer and savoring with them as we discuss challenges and opportunities.

I have to.

Ours is an organization that helps people find meaning, direction, hope and joy in life, and we have to reflect what we yearn to see in the people we serve.

Ours is an organization that encourages peer support among clients at different stages of recovery from substance addiction, and we have to support each other in fostering such healthy peer support environment.

Ours is a strong commitment to make people who feel rejected and abandoned by society feel appreciated and loved again, and we must appreciate and love each other to achieve that.

I often recall the timeless lesson in the biblical account of Peter and John telling a lame man that wanted their alms that they could only give him what they had – which were healing and restoration - and not the alms he wanted and expected. And they did just that; they healed and restored him.

We indeed give others what we have. Love or hate. Fidelity or distrust. Respect or disregard. Help or abandonment. Friendship or antagonism. Attention or avoidance.

So, what do you have?

I am sure you have it in you to be friendly, trusting and trustworthy. Your work – no matter what it is – requires you to be friendly, trusting and trustworthy. People are social beings. They have feelings, they have emotions, they need to be appreciated and respected. They like to have relationships. They like community.

Nobody likes to be alone all the time. Do you? Nobody wants to be without a sense of belonging to at least one group of people. Nobody likes to be treated as inferior or worthless in any group they feel they belong to. And nothing meaningful and enduring can be achieved in the human society without cooperation and collaboration.

You need your colleagues and your colleagues need you. And apart from being members of the same human stock, you all belong to the same organization with the same mission.

Understanding that and acting based on your understanding should make you appreciate, respect and encourage them in their respective tasks.

Every leader in an organization of any size has a responsibility to promote such. Are you a leader in your organization? Then you should have good and commendable footsteps that others are following.

People tend to follow who they trust and trust who they appreciate and appreciate who they understand and understand who they see as paying them needed attention.

Never forget that.

CHAPTER **4** *BE IN TUNE WITH THE MISSION*

"
Efforts and courage are not enough without purpose and direction.

—JOHN F. KENNEDY
35th President of the United States

You may recall that I made use of the phraseology "same organization with the same mission" in the previous chapter. That's because it's very important to the whole idea of enjoying your work again.

You won't enjoy your work if you don't understand and subscribe to your organization's mission – the "what" and "why" of its existence; the purpose it serves and why.

There's no way around it – if you want to be successful and happy. As one aphorism goes, "Surround yourself with those on the same mission as you."

Can you imagine someone doing hip hop dance at a ballet dancing competition and expecting applause, or a prize? Instead, the audience might laugh or boo that person off the stage.

A similar fate may descend on a chorister singing a roots reggae tune while fellow choristers at a widely advertised concert are singing a popular hymn. The chorister might look and sound odd and odious to even some reggae aficionados in the hymn-loving audience. He may however be hailed the next day at a reggae jam.

Why? Because he's in tune with the jam but out of

tune with the hymn of the previous night.

I often tell my trainees and mentees that whether we're working on an individual project or a collective one, our mission should be clear, compelling and consistent. Or else, we will head in the wrong direction, be in the wrong place, face the wrong challenge or have the wrong outcomes.

Though life tries to pull us in different directions, we have to stay focused and do the right thing. No parent will be happy to learn that their child goes playing soccer while his peers are busy in school. It might be good to play soccer to keep fit, but certainly not during school hours when the focus should be on academics.

Everything in life has a time and a place, and every society has its way of dealing with wants, needs and challenges.

Or do you think an immigrant who neither understands nor subscribes to America's strongly held norms of democratic freedoms and rule of law can truly enjoy residency in the country? Living in America and being antithetical to America's democratic freedoms and rule of law is a recipe for sadness, isolation and possibly crime.

Crime? That's right! Some actions – like tax evasion, political thuggery, forceful proselytization, sexual harassment, encroachment on public property, building without pulling a permit, and bribery - that might be overlooked in other countries, especially the developing ones, are considered illegal in the United States and punished accordingly.

However, if the aforementioned immigrant learns to embrace American values and way of life and make the most of them, it becomes relatively easy to enjoy being part of the spectacular American experience.

In other words, the cliché that says "When in Rome, do as Romans do" applies also to the American society. Every society has its own widely accepted way of life and the same is true of organizations like yours.

An organization's mission becomes a way of life when it moves from mere statement on its website or marketing collaterals to plausible and pleasant reality, courtesy of the understanding and diligence of its priceless human assets – the leadership and the staff.

Simply put, a mission is about why and for whom the organization exists, and a mission statement goes beyond that to also indicate how it fulfills such *raison d'etre*.

When I interview candidates for any leadership position, I am keenly interested in knowing whether they clearly understand and appreciate why we exist as a faith-based nonprofit organization. While they may not be able to readily recite our mission statement, it is important they know what we do on daily basis in metro Detroit, and why we do it.

Also important is the need for them to explain to me how their skillset and experience put them in a suitable position to contribute significantly to the continued fulfilment of that mission.

Let me guess. You are wondering if we have had candidates who said all the right things but failed to perform well when the rubber met the road. Of course! Who hasn't?

Some candidates are good in interview stagecraft but bad in rolling up their sleeves and doing the things that make a real difference in the organization and the population it serves. But that should not obliterate the need for everyone to start the journey by knowing and understanding our mission. As the holy book says, "My people perish for lack of knowledge." I agree.

Not knowing the mission of an organization is not knowing how to succeed in that organization, and not knowing how to succeed is an invitation to disappointment and frustration.

That's why we never host an event without giving our staff members, volunteers and donors the opportunity to learn more about our mission or be reminded of it. We do so by bringing former or current clients to speak about how the work of the organization has changed their lives; helping them to find stability, gain sobriety, gain independence by generating steady income and/or become reunited with their loving family and friends.

The audience reaction to our monthly Call To Service luncheon for staff, and annual Graduation Banquet involving community stakeholders says it all. Some sit on the edge of their seats, some clap excitedly, some shed tears of joy, some smile intensely, some shout words of support and commendation.

It's all focused on the mission; our mission. And experience has shown me that when the focus is off such mission, morale plummets and performance and outcome plummet as well.

So, is your morale low at work? Do you feel like you are not making any headway? Are you increasingly feeling dissatisfied and discouraged? Check to see if you are in tune with the mission of your organization. If your understanding of such mission is blurred, get reacquainted with it.

Read more about it in your organization's newsletters, social media posts, news clippings, executive speeches and so on. Ask your colleagues some questions about their memorable experiences at the organization. See the mission in action. Talk with satisfied clients.

If you work at a human service organization such as mine, think of what could happen if people in your target audience don't get the services they depend on. Think of the negative impact it could have on them and the community at large.

I was once asked at a town hall on the eastside of Detroit to explain the significance of my organization, and I responded by saying that if Detroit Rescue Mission were to close its doors today, as many as 2200 women and children, veterans and senior citizens would be on the streets, homeless, hungry and hurting. That's the number of people that depend on the organization every day.

I could sense the unease in the auditorium. There was deafening silence. People exchanged quick glances at each other, and the moderator paused for about 30 seconds before asking "So, you mean 2200 people would be on the streets of Detroit?"

"Yes, they would! They'd have no other place to go for much-needed help. No other organization here has the capacity to absorb them," I said.

It got people in the audience thinking about the difference we make by giving them an idea of what would happen if we were forced by circumstances beyond our control to stop making that difference.

It's all focused on the mission; our mission. The mission of your organization should also be your mission, and if you've taken the wrong exit, as some do at times, you are most likely to feel unhappy and unenthusiastic but it's not too late to get back on the highway with your colleagues.

While there, commit to boosting your productivity, which is focus of the next chapter.

5

"I believe the choice to be excellent begins with aligning your thoughts and words with the intention to require more from yourself.

—OPRAH WINFREY
*World renowned philanthropist,
actress and TV producer*

Yes! You can perform better if you challenge yourself. You have what it takes to perform better at your current assignment. Just put your mind to it and set sail. There may be hitches along the way, but your determination, sense of purpose and expectation of justifiable rewards should help you get there.

I hope you get there soon.

The way I see it, subpar performance at work, any work, should never be acceptable. It hurts both the employee and the employer.

As an author (simply identified by the initials A.B.) cited in a 1698 publication, *The Mystery of Phanaticism*, "a little knowledge is apt to puff up, and make men giddy, but a greater share of it will set them right, and bring them to low and humble thoughts of themselves."

I agree.

I view "same old, same old" productivity the same way A.B. views little knowledge – as puffing people up and making them giddy. Poor performance and stagnation at work soon come to smell like undercooked food in a non-working refrigerator. So does excuse-laced mediocrity and clock-watching underperformance. They are nothing to celebrate.

Yet, I do give second chances even after such behavior, because I believe when given the right motivation, people can do better. The Holy Book tells the instructive story of a disappointed vineyard owner who wanted to cut down a fig tree that hadn't borne fruit in three years. His wise vineyard keeper advised that instead, it be given a grace period of one year, to be fertilized and given the opportunity to bear fruit. And it did.

Many get surprised when I tell them that occasional failure does not bother me, but stagnation does. That's because we can learn from failure.

All of us – irrespective of our designations and responsibilities – are called to be better, to keep improving, to deliver better results. Innovation is not only for the tech industry; innovation is for everyone. Even those working in nonprofit organizations and government agencies.

Smart farmers faced with limited farmlands don't just stop farming or take solace in stagnating; rather, they find cost-effective ways to make the most of their available lands. No farmer derives joy from showing off unfertilized crops or half-full silos. But every farmer relishes lush green crops and silos that are full.

The marketplace of ideas changes every day. That's why hoteliers improve their rooms regularly. That's why academics keep challenging their existing knowledge. That's why auto companies keep making cars more responsive to customers' needs. That's why fast food restaurants are embracing healthy options.

Apple is widely known and its iPhones sell massively around the world. You probably use an iPhone – just like me. Yet, Apple keeps innovating and launching new models in an effort to satisfy its increasingly demanding customers and grow its market share.

Compare the first iPhone model with the latest; it's a huge difference. The company would have gone out of business if it hadn't innovated. There is always a Samsung or Huawei or Sony or LG itching to win over their users. That's called competition. That's how the world works.

So, are you competitive in your field? It's more

than attending a big name college. It's more than years of experience. Tell me about the difference you've made both in your organization and your community. Tell me about the problems you've solved. Tell me about the people – especially young ones – you've mentored, coached and inspired.

Those things can count more than paper qualifications. There are plenty of high achievers without college degrees. When performance improves, when outcome increases, your impact is likely to increase as well. And that's something to be proud and happy about.

I am happy when we give more rehabbed and furnished homes to indigent families in metro Detroit. I am happy when we take food door-to-door to more families in need. I am happy when we take more veterans, senior citizens and teen moms off the inclement streets and out of the dungeons of hopelessness and helplessness. I am happy when more kids from poor neighborhoods enjoy our state-of-the-art camps and dynamic sports and youth development programs.

That happiness is the product of my refusal to be

complacent. I am not superhuman. I am just like you, simply doing my job to ensure that we not only serve people better but also have the funds to do so.

The need is greater today than when I joined Detroit Rescue Mission over two decades ago. There are now more organizations competing for funding from the same sources. We have to innovate. We certainly have to do better.

What about you? Are you conscious of the need to do better? And do you realize the personal and communal benefits of doing better?

In my many years of senior leadership, I have observed that some people feel offended when a younger person or someone who recently joined the organization is given a higher role.

Their reaction is understandable. After all, everyone has the right to want to climb the corporate ladder. Unfortunately, not everyone is ready for the next level.

Many organizational leaders do not think just of academic qualifications and length of service when promoting people. They look for palpable accomplishments and dependability. They believe those who have delivered results before are more likely to deliver them again.

My advice then is simply this: start performing better, and the next level could be yours.

CHAPTER 6

*TAKE CARE
OF THE HOME
FRONT*

"So much of what is best in us is bound up in our love of family, that it remains the measure of our stability because it measures our sense of loyalty. All other pacts of love or fear derive from it and are modeled upon it.

—HANIEL LONG
American author

Lukova

As adults, we wear many hats – professional, social, political, religious. And within our organizations, we perform multiple functions.

I have a friend who is a political analyst, an author, a soccer coach, community advocate, change agent, husband and father. Nothing makes him happier than that last role. He loves spending time with his son – as he should.

Don't get me wrong. He takes his job and community engagements seriously. But the joys and demands of fatherhood inspire him to better create the kind of community he wants his young son to grow up in.

That community – one of social consciousness, engrained love, even-handed opportunity and even-handed justice - starts with the home. It is the microcosm of the macro community.

Organizations – whether brick and mortar or virtual – should be part of the community. Absolutely. But to me, when it comes to community connections, the mother of them all is family.

This one might come as a shocker to you. It's probably not something you'd expect to read from a well known president and CEO in an ultra-competitive work environment.

But it's true.

Now, you may have been told that productivity and promotion are all about how long you stay at work, even beyond normal business hours. You may have developed the habit of staying late at the office, or taking your work home. Sure, this can at times be unavoidable. But my advice is to make sure, if you do, your family members know what's going on.

Explain to them in clear terms why you have to stay longer at work or bring your work home, and promise to make it up to them. And do make it up to them, That's the responsible thing to do. And the right one.

Former first lady Barbara Bush made one powerful statement that I'll never forget. She said "At the end of your life, you will never regret not having passed one more test, winning one more verdict or not closing one more deal. You will regret time not spent with a husband, a child, a friend or a parent."

I agree.

My many years of marriage, fatherhood, and service

in the nonprofit world have taught me that issues at home can affect productivity at work. By the same token, a crisis at work can make home life unpleasant.

No matter how hard we try to extricate one from the other, the two worlds are interwoven, as dependent as the heart is to the brain. That's why I carefully encourage my staff to give needed attention to their home fronts. I don't see how anyone who neglects his or her family – children, spouse, parent(s) – will also not eventually neglect their work.

It's difficult for me to buy the argument that if you take good care of work, the home will take care of itself. You can't divide one from the other. Yes, income from work makes taking care of home life easier, but you also need goodwill from home to take good care of work.

The wise thing to do therefore is to take good care of both. Many who neglect their families for work tend to have lonely, regretful and often sad senior years. Which is why, while I genuinely treat my team members as part of my extended family, I deem it critical to give my family their needed care and love.

Give everyone their due. You've heard the expression "Give to Caesar what is Caesar's and to God what is God's." You may also have heard that we should owe nobody the debt of love. Do you sense a dichotomy? That's the point.

We all wear many hats. We all have different obligations. Being deliberate in attending to them all is very important.

Now, let me make myself a little more vulnerable. If I ever leave home upset, it shows on me at work – as surely as metal shows rust. My team members will notice it, no matter how hard I try to suppress it. And that could affect the mood and flow of work.

What if someone upsets me at work and I make the mistake of carrying it home? It could easily make my family members uncomfortable or worried. That is definitely not good.

This is why I suggest to leave family issues at home and work issues at work. It is easier said than done, I know. Yet, you and I must continue to make better efforts, every God-given day, to enable us enjoy the blessing of both home and work.

We owe it to our community. We owe it to our legacy. We also owe it to our health and wellbeing, which we will discuss in the next chapter.

CHAPTER 7

PAY NEEDED
ATTENTION TO
YOUR HEALTH

"The foundation of success in life is good health: that is the substratum fortune; it is also the basis of happiness. A person cannot accumulate a fortune very well when he is sick.

—P. T. BARNUM
Entertainer, businessman and politician

Even the most health conscious amongst us can get sick once in a while. But a certain type of sickness is becoming increasingly part of the work place – the feigned sickness.

One Monday morning, someone posted a joke on their Facebook page saying some people were busy at that moment thinking of how to call in sick to work, even though they were perfectly healthy. That joke mirrors reality.

Some people do feign sickness in order to absent themselves from the work they are paid to do. Then when serious sickness comes for real, they get agitated and frustrated.

The way I see it, feigning sickness is inviting sickness, and sickness tends to honor invitations.

There's a story of a woman who called in sick to work one day, but within a few hours posted many pictures of herself frolicking at a party, oblivious that her work supervisor was also her Facebook friend. The pictures exposed her lies, and the next day, she lost her job. She fell into depression. And depression is sickness.

Trust me, health is nothing to toy with. A day of

needless no-show at work profits nothing when sickness comes knocking.

Our forefathers were wise when they described health as wealth. And now, we know that health affects our peace and happiness, and its absence can lead to instability and sadness.

Good health enables us to do many things in life, including being punctual and proficient at work. It lets us enjoy our free time and vacations. We can run marathons, take long walks, run around the house with our kids and grandkids – all with good health. Taking care of ourselves may not be cheap, but it is always worth the time, effort and money.

Every employer can share the sadness of highly productive and trusted employees who fell seriously ill and could not fill positions that had once seemed made for them. And you can imagine how frustrated the employees themselves felt.

I still miss former colleagues and employees who fell ill and passed away. I wish they were still here, helping the needy in metro Detroit. That perhaps explains why a few years ago, I hosted a luncheon in their honor, with their family members as special guests. I felt that I had to.

Whenever I hear that a staff member is sick, I wonder if – apart from the health insurance we provide and the regular prayers we encourage – there's any other thing we could do to help them live healthier.

I know the genes play a crucial role in our health as do personal lifestyle and choices but I wish I had the power to stop people from getting sick. I can only offer a few pieces of advice.

In this digital age, many jobs entail sitting for long hours in front of a computer, which could affect one's health, especially as we age. What if one learns to stand and stretch arms and legs for a few minutes? What if one's employer can provide ergonomic chairs, eye-friendly screens and 15-minute exercise breaks?

A reputable medical researcher once told me that genes aside, nutrition is a very important health determinant. We are what – and how – we eat. Yes, healthy foods are more expensive, but so are diseases. Habitually having breakfast and lunch at a fast food near your place of work is not healthy.

So, consider waking up early to have your breakfast, and make lunch to bring to work. It saves you money. It also gives you peace of mind, and might help prolong your life.

Reducing or avoiding intake of sugary sodas, cookies and candies is a good idea for anyone who wants to be healthy enough to enjoy their work and home. I know we are bombarded these days with tempting advertisements on junk food or fast food, but the desire and willingness to be healthy and happy should override such temptations.

Now, here is the big one: not being sensitive to telltale signs our body is giving us. This is a dangerous trait. Why do some of us with good health insurance and who live in close proximity to a hospital wait until it is too late before we visit the doctor? Routine medical checkups are essential, especially when you get past 40.

If discovered early, many aggressive diseases can be properly managed in a way that prolongs life and maintains productivity at work. Prevention is really worth a pound of cure.

Taking care of one's weight is another important

area. So is keeping a positive attitude. If you want to start enjoying your work again, you might want to be holistic about living a good life. As Albert Einstein masterfully put it, "Life is like riding a bicycle. To keep your balance, you must keep moving." Keep making efforts to improve yourself in all areas: thoughts, words and deeds.

It's up to you now.

CONCLUSION

"The chief condition
on which, life, health
and vigor depend on, is
action. It is by action that
an organism develops
its faculties, increases
its energy, and attains the
fulfillment of its destiny.

—COLIN POWELL
*Retired four-star general and
65th U. S. Secretary of State*

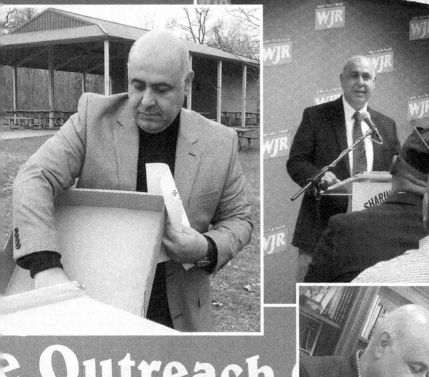

e **Outreach** C

If you've ever felt disrespected by a bank teller, shop attendant, air hostess, physician assistant or nonprofit receptionist, you are not alone. I have felt disrespected, too – more times than I can count.

Chances are that those employees that disrespected you and me are not enjoying their work. Perhaps they don't like the pay. Yet they stay there. As if that's not bad enough, they vent their frustration on the people they are supposed to be courteous to – and by doing so, they hurt their employers.

For a nonprofit like mine, the hurt could come in the form of volunteers, partners and donors drawing the curtains and turning their attention elsewhere. And for a for-profit organization like a bank or fast food, customers may simply take a hike and post negative comments on social media.

So, not enjoying the job you have right now can be a terrible thing. It's like tormenting a decent host family with loud music and filthiness.

Social media is awash with people's disdain for their jobs. Such disdain can severely affect morale in the workplace.

We all love the expression "do what you love" but, frankly, not everyone has that privilege. Not if they need to earn a living. So, a better option is to love what they're doing. Or to paraphrase the holy book, make the most of any legitimate job you find and do your job with commitment and integrity.

Now. What about moving jobs? We may have good reasons to switch employers, but they should never justify treating your current one badly. That's like trying to reach the future by gobbling the present. Prospective employers will often ask about problems you've solved and teams you've built. They may likely want to know why you are leaving your current job. If your answer is simply that you no longer enjoy it, you may inadvertently give the impression that you will one day not enjoy the one they are offering.

It's not that difficult for me to figure out if someone is a job hopper. The resume begins the story, and the interview tells the rest. Employers don't want desk warmers, clock watchers or transient employees.

They want impact-minded employees who will embrace and enjoy their jobs, and work well with colleagues and supervisors.

Are you such an employee? Kudos! If you are not, perhaps the *7 Keys To Enjoying Your Work Again* has helped you toward that position. Of course, it's not enough just to read. To truly enjoy your work again, you have to enter the "doing" zone. Start doing things that will make you enjoy your work and life, and you will soon reap the fruits.

It's not rocket science. And it's not without setbacks. We all will have frustrations.

But that's life. That's work too. We get going. We don't give up. We get better and serve better.

AFTERWORD

Right off the bat, let me congratulate Dr. Chad Audi for writing this valuable book.

As every well-written chapter bears witness, it is a fine gift to all the women and men who power offices and factories around us with their talent, trust and tenacity.

Dr. Audi is a respected member of the metro Detroit community of leaders and has done more than many people in making life better for our less fortunate brothers and sisters.

In writing this book, he demonstrates once again his splendid belief that leadership is not about official titles but rather about helping others succeed.

I have followed Dr. Audi's work for many years, and was quite pleased when in the later part of 2014, he invited me to be among his organization Detroit Rescue Mission's first transformation ambassadors. I accepted to serve in such an advisory role because I knew that with Dr. Audi at the helm, it would be like going "from strength to strength."

And my reaction wasn't different when he asked me in December 2018 to write this Afterword, which I consider an honor.

As someone who has been in law enforcement for decades, I know firsthand that worker morale is one of the most important determinants of effective law enforcement.

When morale is high, performance tends to be equally high. But when it is low, productivity suffers and the community bears the brunt. So, an essential part of my job as a police chief is to keep the morale of my men and women high.

The same applies to leaders in other work places, be they public or private. That's why many tech companies,

Dr. Audi getting things done.

especially those located in the Silicon Valley, emphasize worker engagement, motivation and satisfaction. They have employee-friendly work schedules and campuses that attract and retain different shades and forms of talents, from high-energy millennials to highly experienced seniors.

Whether every organization can follow the Silicon Valley example is an issue best suited for another forum. But there is no gainsaying the fact that employees are the heartbeat of every organization and deserve to enjoy the work they do.

That's the thrust of this commendable work, which empowers workers to prioritize and pursue their own motivation.

Traditionally, the responsibility of ensuring worker motivation has been squarely placed on the shoulders of employers but in this book, Dr. Audi says employees also have a huge stake in ensuring their own motivation, which he calls "enjoying your work".

I agree, and I am hopeful you will agree as well after reading this handy book.

Dr. Audi, as an employer, uses the same methods

he advocated in this book. He knows that to succeed in motivating his employees, he has to ensure his own morale is high as well.

So, moving forward, I will continue to motivate the men and women who work under me, and I will also motivate myself using the methods brilliantly canvassed in this book.

ANTHONY HOLT
Associate Vice President & Chief of Police
Wayne State University, Detroit

Dr. Chad Audi

ABOUT THE AUTHOR

Dr. Chad Audi is widely regarded in business and social impact sectors as a visionary and dynamic leader and sought-after business training consultant. His daily work of providing help and hope to the underprivileged and underserved of metro Detroit has been recognized by U.S. presidents, U.S. Congress, state and county governments and city mayors.

Since 2004, he has served as an accomplished President and CEO of Detroit Rescue Mission, a leading nonprofit that runs social enterprises, provides skills development and job readiness training services and is rated by the *U.S. News and World Report* as the 13th largest inpatient, outpatient alcohol, substance abuse treatment and rehab center in the U.S. Under his leadership, the 1909-founded human services organization grew to become the largest rescue mission in the United States, serving an average of 2200 persons a day, with a staff of about 300 and volunteers in excess of 13,000 annually.

An expert of the United Nations Security Council Affairs Division (SCAD), Dr. Audi is a hands-on, proactive troubleshooter who can rapidly identify hard-charging or hidden problems, formulate decisive plans of action, and drive needed change, all within a challenging environment with diverse groups of people.

He earned his master's degree in Finance from Walsh College of Accountancy and Business Administration, and bagged his first Ph.D. in Business Management and Leadership and the second doctorate in Business Administration. He is an active member of many financial, accounting, management and fundraising professional organizations and an author of numerous research papers and articles on management of business and nonprofit.

NOTES

NOTES

CPSIA information can be obtained
at www.ICGtesting.com
Printed in the USA
BVHW041001151019
561050BV00022BA/1087/P